Apostle of Mercy
Fr. Jean-Baptiste Rauzan

Founder of the Fathers of Mercy

The Very Reverend Jean-Baptiste Rauzan
(1757-1847)

Fr. Raymond Borcino S.P.M.

Apostle of Mercy

Fr. Jean-Baptiste Rauzan

Edited by Members of the Fathers of Mercy

Fathers of Mercy
2019

Copyright © 2019 by the Fathers of Mercy

ISBN 978-0-359-79125-5

Fathers of Mercy
806 Shaker Museum Road
Auburn, KY 42206

Cum Permissu Superioris

The Author

Reverend Raymond F. Borcino, S.P.M.

✦✦✦

Over the centuries, men and women have been inspired by the example of those in the Catholic Church who have walked the path of holiness before them. Inspiration is drawn from the knowledge of persons who have charmed and elevated mankind by their works, glorified countries by their genius, and done honor to their race by virtuous deeds. These individuals have followed in the footsteps of Jesus Christ, and heeded His mandate to "go and teach all nations."(Mathew 28:19) However, without proper publicity, those of this character will go undiscovered by future generations.

Until recent years, the life of a zealous French priest, Jean-Baptiste Rauzan, was known only to his contemporaries and the members of the Societies he founded. He is not often mentioned in history. However, despite the comparative obscurity of his life, he was visibly raised up by God for the good of the Church. Together with other founders of religious institutes of his time, he belongs to that galaxy of Apostles who raised, revised, and reconstructed Christian France after the terrible destruction of the French Revolution. Pope Pius VIII said, with gentle liveliness: "You are that good Rauzan about whom I have heard so many admirable things. May the blessing of God be with you."[1]

The Founder of the Society of the Fathers of Mercy was born in circumstances similar to those recognized by the Church for their holiness. His family was wealthy, associating with eminent gentry, and practicing law professionally. As founders of religious communities had done before him, Fr. Rauzan willingly dedicated his wealth and extraordinary talents to propagating the truths of God's mercy and helping the poor. His life was committed to fulfilling the revealing words of Isaias: "The Spirit of the Lord is upon me, wherefore, He hath anointed me to preach the gospel to the poor, He hath sent me to heal the contrite of heart." (Isaiah 61:1)

Jean-Baptiste Rauzan was born in the city of Bordeaux, France, on December 5, 1757, the eldest of the four sons and three daughters of Monsieur Rauzan and Madeleine Maleville. The character of this family was thoroughly religious. This was evidenced by the fact that the youngest son, Belisle, also entered the service of the Church following the example of his brother Jean-Baptiste. Fr. Belisle died a Canon of Bordeaux after leading a life of dedication to priestly ideals and service to the Catholic people of France.

Jean-Baptiste made his first Communion in the Church of St. James in Bordeaux. The precocious maturity of his mind, and more importantly the admirable purity of his heart, let him worthily appreciate this first call of Christ. The continual nourishment he received from the Holy Eucharist would strengthen him for his apostolic endeavors in the turbulent times to come. Many years later, Fr. Rauzan found St. James Church, which he loved so much, profaned by the sons of the Revolution and had to wipe out the traces of sacrilege that plagued this sacred place. With the financial help and devotion of his brothers, Jean-

Baptiste rebuilt the altar and utilized it in the glorious revival of Religion in France.

From his early youth he received a solid Christian education. His early school days began under the guidance of the Jesuits, until they were suppressed. In high school, he established an honor and a name as a student of science.[2] He was a good student, and advanced in the sacred sciences with great piety and devotion. Moreover, the position of honor and the wealth of his family did not dissuade the young student from his anxious desire to give himself most generously to God in the Priesthood.

This priestly vocation was enflamed by a sodality called the Association of Friends, in which Fr. Rauzan would learn to cultivate a strong inner life. The basis of the sodality was directed toward prayer, works of charity, and devotion to the Blessed Virgin Mary. He was initiated in prayer, Christian doctrine, and in good works. Each month, the Association would choose a specific virtue to put into particular practice during the respective liturgical season and special devotions. The sodality would also emphasize sanctification through the union existing between the members, which Fr. Rauzan would later adapt to the societies of religious life that he would found. Through the training received in the Association of Friends, Jean Baptiste would find the source of his priestly vocation, and the motivation for his future apostolic activity.

Jean-Baptiste's father desired and hoped that his eldest son would study law. For a time, Jean-Baptiste did begin the necessary studies in this field, but soon added to these the study of Theology. Through constant devotion to prayer and application of work, he persuaded his father to give consent to enter formally the seminary conducted by the Disciples of St. Vincent De Paul. All his life Jean-Baptiste kept a very lively and grateful affection for the family of St. Vincent and for those Missionary Priests "…in whom Pontiffs found advice, the scholars found guides, the Church found martyrs, and the poor friends. Men brought together by humility, led by the most active charity, animated by the spirit of mortification. Men who were not revolted by the rudest and the most revolting kind of work."[3]

After entering the seminary, he received the order of tonsure on April 4, 1778 by the Bishop of Agent, in the Church of Notre-Dame de Bordeaux. Successively, he received all the necessary minor Orders and was ordained to the Priesthood on May 25th, 1782. Two years later, he presented to the University of Bordeaux his dissertation for a doctorate in Theology. His esteem at the University was such that he had his thesis approved without any examination. He had worked under the direction of Fr. Jean Langoiran, Vicar General of Bordeaux. Eight years later, in 1792, Fr. Langoiran and one of his companions, Fr. Louis Dupuy, were the first to shed their blood in Bordeaux in the evil days when godlessness was preparing France for destruction.

Immediately after his ordination to the sacred priesthood, Fr. Rauzan was not assigned to any specific work of the diocese of Bordeaux. He lived with his family in the parish of St. Colombe. It was during this time that he was assigned to the training of young men in the study of philosophy at the College de Guyenne. Fr. Rauzan aimed at fortifying these men against the errors of the day. He used to have the students meet several times a week at his father's house. Forcefully and brilliantly, they would refute the ideas disseminated by Voltaire, Rousseau and Diderot. The young men were encouraged to attend Daily Mass and receive the Sacrament of Penance at least once a month. Stemming from his foundation of prayer and study, Fr. Rauzan's earliest days as a priest focused on catechesis and evangelization.

His first assignment was to the church of Saint Projet. There, his simplicity, his reserve, his devotion and his talents began to achieve esteem. He soon gained the respect of the people, and his dynamic preaching became a great asset. People from all parts of the city came to hear him preach, and the poor beat a path to his door for consolation and help. His concern for the poor demanded that he kept a collection of ready-made clothes. When someone came for clothing, he would give a little talk on the love of God and send the individual home, proud of their new attire.

The Archbishop of Bordeaux soon learned of the goodness of the young priest, especially of his talents for teaching. The Archbishop had a small seminary in his diocese, but was looking for a young, mature priest to direct the students attending this school. Fr. Rauzan became his choice and Rauzan was sent to the Seminary called St. Raphael. This was a hard sacrifice to make for the priest with a shepherd's heart, but he was accustomed from early life to conquer all difficult tasks. In this new environment, he distinguished himself again by the clarity of teaching and knowledge. The Archbishop set aside a professorship in theology for him at the University of Bordeaux, but Fr. Rauzan never accepted the position. At the insistence of the people of his former parish, St. Projet, he returned to parish duties with the blessing of his Archbishop, to the delight of his people.

In this time, Fr. Jean-Baptiste devoted himself to the study of preaching. In order to learn the style and doctrinal content necessary for effective delivery, he visited Paris and surrounding cities to hear the best preachers of the day. He was not satisfied with the sermons delivered in the local churches. To him, sermons of the day had become more philosophical than Christian, more academic than Catholic. They contained very little doctrine, emphasizing more of a dry and tilted style. His application to the duties of preaching, matched with the desire to win souls, reaped results. His success was only for a short time, however, for a new philosophy was winning ground in France.

�֤ ✤ ✤

In 1792, the storm that had been building for a century burst over France with an intense fury. Well does a historian describe it:

> Thus, from ripples of skepticism towards the end of the seventeenth century a great wave of unbelief swept over Europe in the eighteenth, to crest and break in the utter Atheism of the French Revolution. Headed by the infamous Apostate Voltaire, a group of rationalist writers published an "Encyclopedia", which, pretending to be a summary of modern knowledge, carried, scattered through it, articles attaching Catholic beliefs and ideals with the weapons of scoffer and ridicule. Along with the work of another Rationalist "philosopher", Jean Jacques Rousseau, the "Encyclopedia" did much to undermine the Faith in France and pave the way for the Revolution.[4]

From July 12, 1790, the priests of France were required to accept the Civil Constitutions of the Clergy. The faithful priests were forced to go, either into hiding, or to escape to foreign soil and await the day when they would be again permitted to return and unite the faithful. Jean-Baptiste refused to take the schismatic oath of the Civil Constitution, and upon the advice of higher authority left his beloved France for England on July 22, 1792. At the moment the ship was ready to sail, a search party almost captured him. Later in his life, when another storm broke over France, he remained impassible in the midst of bullets that rained about him.

He remained in London about a year, constantly occupied with supporting and strengthening the faith of his fellow Frenchmen. He dedicated his time to catechesis, evangelization and prayer. In addition, he would regularly hold conferences with Protestant ministers on points that separated them from the truths of the Catholic Faith.

In 1793, Fr. Jean-Baptiste went to Belgium. In this country, by Divine Providence, he became associated with a wise adviser and devoted friend, Fr. Augé, later to become a member of the Missionaries of France and the Society of the Fathers of Mercy. In Antwerp, Fr. Rauzan again became known for his preaching, especially on the topic of Providence. His activities in Belgium were some of the first great events of Fr. Rauzan's life as a missionary. His emphasis on Divine Providence during this time manifested a great faith and total commitment of himself to the hands of God.

Fr. Rauzan's work in Belgium soon came to an end due to the entrance of the Republican Armies. He was driven into Germany and after a short stay in Munster and Dusseldorf, he settled in Berlin. Preaching was not all that occupied his days. Fr. Rauzan would often gather young Catholics together for meetings. He would serve them breakfast, lead them in services, take a walk, and hear their confessions. He would also recommend different books to read. The guidance of consciences, instructions and good works filled the greater part of his time of exile.

Fr. Rauzan spent eight years in foreign lands before the news came that the time was ripe to return to France. At last, the faithful were to have the word of God preached to them and the joy of kneeling before their altars once again. Fr. Rauzan took up residence with a friend close to the Palace of Justice Square and would go to preach at the Carmelite Church that had been a witness to the scenes of martyrdom. His ministry in Paris consisted of preaching, teaching catechism, and caring for the young. As the reputation of his preaching grew from day to day, he soon found himself connected with personalities of high honor. When the Concordat of 1801 had been promulgated, returning to the Church some of her rights, the voice of the people sought to have Fr. Rauzan raised to the Episcopate. Scarcely had he heard these rumors when his humility inspired him with fear. This may have been a motive that caused him to want to leave for Bordeaux. However, in 1802, the newly appointed Archbishop of Bordeaux, Msgr. Francis D'Aviau, had different plans for him.

Archbishop D'Aviau had only been installed in his See a short time when the former Archbishop, Msgr. De Cice arrived from England. After an interview, the former Archbishop gave his successor valuable instructions about the clergy of the Diocese. When he came to speaking about Fr. Rauzan he did so in such high terms, that the new Archbishop thought that it would be fitting to have Jean-Baptiste read the Bull of Institution on the day that he took possession of his See.

The ceremony, which was so consoling to the faith of the people of Bordeaux, was arranged for the Feast of the Assumption, 1802. For the first time in years, the priests arrived to meet the new Archbishop and dared to walk in the streets in their priestly robes. In the church dedicated to the Blessed Virgin Mary, before a select audience, Fr. Rauzan read the Pontifical Bull. The new Archbishop was very pleased with the beautiful sermon given by Fr. Rauzan. "There isn't a priest in the diocese who has obtained," he said, "more of a reputation because of his talents and virtue." [5]

Fr. Rauzan was also made honorary Vicar-General. This title was only honorary due to the members of the government being fearful that he would exercise too powerful an influence in favor of the Church. Therefore, they refused to grant the Archbishop's petition to have him raised to the office of Vicar-General of the diocese.

In his duties, the Archbishop assigned Fr. Rauzan to inspect five sections of the diocese surrounding the city of Bordeaux and to report on the conditions of the faithful, churches and the clergy. Fr. Rauzan applied himself to the fulfillment of this assignment. Being tireless in his zeal, he often had to brave government officials of revolutionary memories who opposed the work of God, or people who had been indoctrinated with false teachings and had set themselves up in some of the churches of the diocese.

In his report, Fr. Rauzan recounted the condition of places where churches were opened and the Revolution had scarcely been weeded out. In many churches, there were not any confessionals, pulpits, baptisteries or altars. In the rectories, there was desolation. Those who lived in them often had to go and beg for a piece of bread from poor farmers or workers, so great was their misery. Yet, there were still some devoted parishes who had maintained the faith and had never let schism obtain a foothold. There were other parishes where the constitutional priests who were extremely easy-going would not give up either the rectory or the church. The result of the inquiry: "A great deal of evil, and not much of good."[6]

Immediately the Archbishop began the work of rebuilding his diocese. He re-established the ceremonies of worship, enforced wise rulings, granted foundations for religious houses, revived apostolic preaching, built pastoral retreats as well as a small seminary and started new schools. Fr. Rauzan took an active part in this most prominently by preaching the Jubilee Lenten services of 1804 in Paris. When opportunity presented itself in his ministry opportunities, he also would conduct catechism classes for the children, preparing them for their First Communion. In 1836, when Fr. Rauzan was seventy-nine and came to Bordeaux for the last time, many of his former students would caution his companions and tell them: "Take good care of Father. He is a saint. We owe the feelings of piety that are our joy to his catechism classes."[7]

A series of sermons in Paris during 1805 brought new recognition to Fr. Rauzan. In 1806, a Lenten series in Lyon opened for Fr. Rauzan a new and glorious career. It was because of this series that his talents, ability, and priestly manner came to the attention of Cardinal Fesch, Archbishop of Lyon. This Prelate, the uncle of Emperor

Napoleon, by his position of dignity and family heritage wielded power and opportunity for the restoration of Religion in France. Desirous of France's return to the glories of Catholicism, and being a man of sincerity, the cardinal used his abilities for the purpose of the propagation of the Faith.

The Cardinal requested the Archbishop of Bordeaux to grant the release of Fr. Rauzan. He would begin the work in October if only Fr. Rauzan could be permitted to be in charge of the new work and establishment. If, however, Fr. Rauzan was not permitted to undertake the mission, the work must be abandoned. The Archbishop, of course, was not in favor of giving his beloved friend to the work, but when the Cardinal insisted, and finally petitioned for a loan of Fr. Rauzan, the good Archbishop of Bordeaux consented.

In the month of May 1807, the Cardinal installed the head of the missions in the house on the hill of La Croix Rousse, in the northern suburb of Lyons. At the same time, Fr. Rauzan was named Canon of the Metropolitan See, a Member of the Council of the Archbishop and honorary Vicar-General. Fr. Rauzan did not wish to have these honors accorded to him because he had often expressed the desire to do all things for the glory of the Church. In undertaking this work, he did not wish any salary or any temporal advantage for himself, but he did petition for all the necessary funds to be able to compensate the efforts of others. He wished the liberty of choosing his co-workers because he only wished to have those who were poor in spirit, those who practiced mortification and were perfectly obedient. Fr. Rauzan did choose many friends and men of apostolic love. Many joined him in this new work, and Fr. Rauzan was happy that the project was in operation. This new endeavor in the year 1808 would prove to be the foundation of the Congregation of the Fathers of Mercy.

Success was given to the apostolic missions immediately. Even the Emperor Napoleon expressed his pleasure in the work. The great graces sought after seemed to be filling the hearts of the faithful. A few years, however, can bring many changes. The work was growing, but there was also a new storm rising which would sweep across France and cause the cessation of the missions. Pope Pius VII and Napoleon were at odds. The Holy Father finally had to draw the line and informed Napoleon that he would not grant any concessions contrary to his duty. The Pope had been deprived of his States and even of his freedom, and so decided that he would no longer submit to the demands of the Emperor. Exasperated, the Emperor let his wrath fall upon the clergy. An imperial decree, with one blow, demolished the recently re-established societies of religious life, including the work of Fr. Rauzan.

The factors which brought about the cessation of the good work had backgrounds and foundations in the deprivation of the rights and honors of the Holy Father. The Holy Father, Pius VII, passed a verdict against the invalidity of the marriage of the Emperor's brother, Jerome, and this coupled with the Pope's refusal to co-operate in the exclusion of England from European trade angered the Emperor. In May 1809, the Papal States were seized by French troops and annexed to the French Empire. The excommunication of Napoleon that followed took little effect. The Holy Father was taken prisoner and brought to Savona, the main body of Cardinals being brought to Paris.

Soon after, Fr. Rauzan was appointed by Cardinal Fesch to act as chaplain to the Emperor. The duty caused him much hardship and worry. Napoleon desired dissolution of his own marriage with Josephine in order to marry Marie-Louise of Austria. The Holy Father had not pronounced on the validity of Napoleon's first marriage, and many of the Cardinals were divided as to what should be done. However, on January 9, 1810, the Official of Paris, rendered a decision by which the marriage contracted between Emperor Napoleon and Empress Josephine, without the presence of the required witnesses and the proper pastor, was declared null.

Fr. Rauzan spent the next three years in Paris studying, guiding consciences, preaching retreats, and performing good works. He encouraged Madam de Lezeau in the foundation of the Order of the Mother of God and in the work of orphans, which was later adopted by the Emperor and became the House of Orphans of the Legion of Honor.

Finally, Napoleon went down in defeat. On June 4, 1814, the new King Louis XVIII granted a charter declaring the Catholic Religion the religion of the state. The government showed good intention and the Church in France began to have hope. Fr. Rauzan was appointed

Chaplain to the King and began again the work of bringing religion to the interior of France. His venerable Prelate, Cardinal Talleyrand-Perigord called upon him to preach the Season of Advent at the Court. There he had his usual success, but instead of using the occasion to step higher, he thought of a new mission society.

Fr. Rauzan began his plans for the society which would be dedicated to missions and would not be confined to one diocese of the country. A young priest associated himself with Fr. Rauzan in the work. This priest had generously given up all the prestige that was his from noble birth, a magnificent fortune, and a scholarly education, to dedicate himself to the missions. In 1814, Fr. de Forbin-Janson, the young priest whom Fr. Rauzan had accepted, went to Rome and made known the plan of Fr. Rauzan to the Holy Father. He was advised to return to France and instruct the people, give missions for the laity, and conduct retreats for the clergy.

The new Society, called the "Society of the Missionaries of France," was approved by diocesan authorities on January 9, 1815, and soon after by King Louis XVIII. The work of the Society was widely commended for its invaluable contribution to the spiritual regeneration of the nation during the period of the Restoration and to it belongs the credit for France's later preeminence as the most mission-minded country of Europe.[8]

The first mission, conducted by the members of the new Society, was in the city of Beauvais. It was a grand success. These new missionaries of evangelization became an efficacious means to draw people back to the principles of religion and wisdom. However, the missionary life was cut short by the return of Napoleon and the "hundred days" of strife.

After the reign of Napoleon completely ended, Fr. Rauzan and his group of missionaries received invitations from the Bishops of all the great cities of France and they tried to fulfill them. Yet, in the midst of this great spiritual revival, many members of the Society so distinguished themselves by their devotion and learning, that they were in constant demand and almost wore themselves out to fulfill their duties. Fr. Fayet distinguished himself in preaching and personal spirituality. His talents and piety became so well known that he was elevated to the Bishopric of Orleans. Fr. de Forbin-Janson was made bishop of Nancy and Toul and Primate of Lorraine. His missionary life, however, did not terminate with his appointment to a diocese.

In 1816, Louis XVIII gave possession of Mont-Valerian to the Missionaries of France. Since 1556, this had been a chapel located on top of a hill and there had been erected a Calvary scene. For many years hermits lived there, but at the time of the French Revolution, all the priests had been sent away. This place of prayer and penance was transformed into an abode of pleasure; one of the Calvary chapels was dedicated to Venus. When Fr. Rauzan took possession of the property, he immediately turned it into a house of retreat and conducted novenas in honor of the Passion and Sufferings of Christ. High on the hill was erected a cross which could be seen from all parts of Paris. From its vantage point, it would attract all eyes, dispel indifference, bring light to the ignorant, and crush impious sarcasm. It would be an imposing and solemn profession of faith for royalty and peasantry adoring the Word Incarnate, Who died on the cross for the salvation of the world.

From 1815 until the Revolution of 1830, it was a profitable time and a most rewarding era for Fr. Rauzan. He organized many associations in the good city of Orleans. An organization of men was formed to visit and instruct the prisoners. The Ladies of Providence was re-established for the purpose of maintaining the House of the Good Shepherd for penitent women. A young ladies organization was formed at first for relief of the poor, but later they created the Orphanage of the Holy Childhood, which had been established by Bishop de Forbin-Janson. The example of Orleans was imitated successfully in most of the cities where Fr. Rauzan conducted his missionary activities.

The holy and renowned Fr. Rauzan had a reputation for the practice of many virtues, but one of his finest was the love of children. He desired to guide them by study and the knowledge of Our Blessed Lord to a sublime eternal happiness. He helped to advance the cause of education either by some work he organized in connection with education, or by applying educational principles, new or old, for the purpose of more effective results. It cannot be said, however, that many of the ideas he expounded in behalf of Christian education originated with him, but many of the methods already in use or established, benefitted by his foresight for proper application.

His life, in a manner, echoes the lives of St. Ignatius de Loyola and St. John Baptist de la Salle. Each man lived at the transition of their respective centuries and brought about restoration or transformations in society at the beginning of the next century. They did not come from poor families, yet their lives were devoted to the poor in diverse ways. The three were born amidst events most stirring and significant. They were founders of religious societies, which would be instrumental for the advancement of education.

Fr. Rauzan was an astute and keen observer. By attending the different churches in Paris to listen to the renowned preachers of the day, he learned and retained mentally the most important factors and aptitudes of good teaching and preaching. He was an investigator and a scientific educator; always searching for the new, better, and effective way of teaching. The presentation of Catholic truths and the exposition of them with clarity permit a good teacher to turn into ordinary language his vast store of learning in order to make it more attractive.

Fr. Rauzan's intimate friendships with, and the many delicate tasks entrusted to him by outstanding people are an indication of the respect and high regard conferred upon him. He was an artisan of peace, mercy and faith and he made others happy. He possessed a love of books, never divorcing himself from studies and meditation. He had intellectual virtues tempered with prudence. He was endowed with rare gifts of grace and nature. He was most dynamic, in the sense that he could sway very large groups. He was a student of eloquence, with a delivery and subject matter that were always influential. He attracted others by his kindness, modesty, simple manner and understanding. He was not to write extensive works or many formal treatises on the educational problems, but he possessed an insight into the proper and Christian philosophy of education.

Fr. Rauzan was devoted to the ideals of intellectual and moral training. He kept the method and the life of Christ burning in his very soul. The chief almoner to the King entrusted to Fr. Rauzan and his Society of the Missions, the community of the Clerks of St. Denis Chapter. In a sense, this was a Minor Seminary made up of select students intended for service of the Grand Almoner and the Missions.

A hallmark of Fr. Rauzan's teaching style was to make his lectures timely, as well as valuable, so that the hearers expressed his ideas and thoughts in action. His time and age needed master-teachers, for men were fearful to speak the truth and live for the truth. In those days, when man needed the message of Christ, it meant that teacher and student had to be one in the study of the life of Christ and the practical application of the Gospel. A message of hope and love was necessary to the world. In the seminary, the teacher had to mold the lives of the students in order that they might become men of knowledge, of dignity, of strength, of poise, of humility, attain a forgetfulness of self, and have a love of Christ that pervaded all their actions in which Christ is supreme.

A common mistake and a false opinion which seemed to be adopted at the time was that explanation of the catechism and teaching the doctrines of the Church did not need a trained teacher or catechist of outstanding talents; that is, teaching could be entrusted indifferently to any Catholic instructed in the main truths of religion. Fr. Rauzan saw the fallacy of such shortsighted thinking. The unskilled to him were the drudges of the work yards, where sentiment did not flourish any more benevolence and understanding. The victims of these unqualified teachers found study to be more difficult and in spite of persevering and desperate efforts, floundered in a quandary of confusion.

Fr. Rauzan knew human nature with all its passions, all its defects, all its whims and fancies. His philosophy of education did not touch extremes, but was tempered by a note of sane optimism. He did not assume that man's nature was perfect; neither did he condemn it as corrupt. He knew that man was suffering from the wound inflicted by Adam's sin; but he was confident that with the help of Christ's sacramental forces, in the bright sunshine of Divine Grace, human nature could regain its health and grow up to mental and moral maturity

Fr. Rauzan was a man of good taste; a teacher of elegance and a devotee of the art of teaching. He advocated the noble ideals of family association of teacher and student, that the teacher should be a person of dominance with the singular union of knowledge and quality.

Fr. Rauzan was always animated with a richness for the love of God. He believed that love proved itself more by works than by words. A vocation to teaching requires many virtues. There must be present a firm desire to succeed. Fr. Rauzan often motivated others in the perfection of teaching with the desire for zeal. The difficulty of success does not stop real devotion; it inflames it. The spirit of fervor, along with the desire to sanctify oneself and others, provided it is nourished with the spirit of prayer, will win the blessing of God and the grace of accomplishment.

From the earliest years of his apostolic labors, Fr. Rauzan became most interested in the education of the women of France. To him the education of women was the most powerful influence for saving society. Women should have a great number of virtues and a great deal of education. Providence helped Fr. Rauzan in this fulfillment when Madame Desfontaines came to him for advice in setting up a religious congregation devoted to the education of young women. Madame Desfontaines opened a school for the boarding of children and decided to give it more consistency by setting up a religious congregation devoted to the education of youth, especially young women. In order to receive help in her endeavors and seek the blessing of God, she decided to make a Novena at Mont-Valerian.

On September 29, 1820, Madame Desfontaines was determined to meet the aged priest whom she had heard giving a talk to some soldiers. She was attracted to this servant of God, and when they settled down to a discussion of her problems she learned to her great surprise that this priest had been nourishing the same noble thoughts in his mind for some time, with the sincere hope that God would send him some means which would help his ideas bear fruit.

Although Fr. Rauzan was burdened with many labors, he gave the petition of Madame Desfontaines much thought and consideration. However, he did not agree to accept the responsibility of having Madame Desfontaines place the entire foundation of her Congregation in his hands. She kept urging him to lend his assistance and even went to see the Cardinal in order to have him intercede with Fr. Rauzan, thereby making known the conditions under which he would help with the foundation.

After six months of meditation and prayer, Fr. Rauzan drew up the rule for the Congregation. While it sacrificed some of the exteriors of the religious state, it kept the spirit and the virtues, which are characteristic of true spouses of Jesus Christ. Madame Desfontaines accepted the complete new rule of Fr. Rauzan. She had the happiness of seeing her Community approved by the Church and authorized by the government. Cardinal de Perigord on April 6, 1821 approved the Statues of the Congregation, and within a short space of time, four members made a retreat under Fr. Rauzan. The ceremony of Profession was held on the 16th of August, 1821. The name of St. Clotilde was chosen for the congregation in honor of the pious Queen, to whom the country owed its faith, and who helped reawaken religion in France through the education of women.

Madame Desfontaines died three months later, but Fr. Rauzan manifested the intention of taking care of the institution until it was imbued with the proper spirit. For two years, he followed the work of the Sisters with extreme solicitude and untiring effort. For the rest of his life, he kept in communication with the Order of St. Clotilde. He assigned one of the priests of his Society to remain with them and constantly give direction and assistance.

In the month of September 1824, Louis XVIII died. Fr. Rauzan was invited to preach the funeral oration for the King. The subject was a difficult one, but he already had experience in sermons that had to be treated with delicacy and propriety. The new King, Charles X, pursuing the same Catholic policy as his predecessor, tried to have the irreligious literature flooding the country halted. He had some success because he had made sacrilegious and irreligious writing criminal offenses. He further gave the clergy control in education, but restricted them in general. Accordingly, when the next Revolution came in July 1830, the clergy again received the full force of the blow.

✠✠✠

The Missionaries of France organized and directed by Fr. Rauzan had no formal bond of vows at the time of the Revolution of 1830, when they were forced to seek shelter in diocesan activities and other apostolic works. The missionary society had been established as a "free association," allowing members to leave when duties required their services elsewhere. Charity was the bond which held the Missionaries to the spirit of restoration of Religion in France, and which ignited the spark of Faith. The Revolution of 1830 caused all missionary activity to cease. This zealous priest was truly distressed, but did not lose his strong hope and determination. He had been in battle before. He had learned many lessons of history and realized that the Church is never fatally wounded. When the clouds of Revolution were darkest, Fr. Rauzan cultivated and nourished the brightest plans for the future.

Shortly before the beginning of new disorders and the start of the outbreak in July 1830, five priests of the Missionaries of France requested and obtained permission to be united by vow. Others did not wish to bind themselves as yet, because they did not believe that the organization was permanent and complete. Fr. Rauzan, however, desired to plant the first seeds of a new community and approved those who wished to be united by vow. Like St. Ignatius and six of his companions who assembled in the Chapel of St. Denis on the hill of Montmartre, so too, did Fr. Rauzan and five of his companions assemble in the lower Chapel of St.

Genevieve, where they secretly pronounced the vows of Stability, Obedience and Chastity before the altar of the Blessed Virgin Mary.

However, it was not long before the property belonging to the Missionaries was destroyed by thieves and vandals as a result of the new revolution. Fr. Rauzan was convinced that a new era was in store for France and the Society. His life was threatened by revolutionaries, and the government took back the ordinance by which Louis XVIII had authorized the Society of the Missionaries of France. Thus, he turned his heart and eyes toward Rome.

When the new storm of the Second Revolution in 1830 came, he decided to go to Rome to visit the Holy Father and make plans for the future. He sent two of his missionaries ahead to make preparations. On October 11, Fr. Rauzan arrived in Rome. His joy was increased upon meeting his confreres, but it was completely fulfilled in an audience with Pope Pius VIII. They discussed the trouble in France and the work of the missions. Fr. Rauzan left the audience filled with emotion and gratitude.

Rome opened the doors of welcome to this gracious and humble French priest. His sympathy was confined to no age, no class, however obscure or oppressed. None was beneath his regard. He had a deep instinct, a God-given intuition of universal brotherhood. He was interested in his fellow men; how they lived, acted, suffered and struggled.

While in Rome, the Dominican Friars extended a cordial reception to Fr. Rauzan. They gave him for his use, an apartment in the Minerva Monastery. From 1818, the

Society of the Missionaries of France desired to enter a holy and cordial union of good works and prayers with this distinguished Order of the Church. Fr. Rauzan, during his stay in Rome, accomplished this union and received final affiliation with the Order from the Master General. It was given on November 5th, 1848.

Fr. Rauzan was present in Rome when the Holy Father Pius VIII died. The Cardinals arrived in Rome and went into Conclave. He had the pleasure of visiting with several of the Cardinals, especially the Prefect for the Propaganda of the Faith, Cardinal Capelleri. On February 2nd, the election was over, Cardinal Capelleri succeeded Pius VIII under the name of Gregory XVI. The friendship of Fr. Rauzan and the new Pope continued and waxed stronger in mutual admiration and help.

Apostolic life is a life of sacrifice, and in order for the sacrifice to be perfect, there must be a giving of one's self, irrevocably and for all time, and to fulfill this there must be a vow and a rule. Fr. Rauzan went to Rome with his outlined constitutions and a strong desire to complete them at the tomb of the Apostles. Three years were devoted to revising and completing the Constitution of a society to be called the "Society of the Priests of Mercy under the Patronage of the Immaculate Conception." This new Society would be under the control of the Propagation of the Faith, since there was a special closeness between the foreign missions and home missions.

During this time of formulating the Constitutions, Fr. Rauzan frequently was seen kneeling before the altar of the Blessed Virgin in the Church of Minerva, pleading with Our Blessed Lord, through the Virgin Mary, for light from on high. The new Society would be completely indebted to the Blessed Virgin in the fruits of apostolic ministry. Through her intercession, Fr. Rauzan acquired, more and more, the practical conviction of those beautiful maxims that he bequeathed to his children.

In France, the cloud on the religious horizon was beginning to lift. Fr. Rauzan's confreres, who had remained in France, sent him numerous requests to return. He decided to rally the members of his Society in order to renew the preaching of the Divine Word. Turning this thought over in his mind, he visited the Vatican. Pope Gregory received him with cheerful simplicity and listened to his desire to return to France. When leaving he asked the Holy Father for approval of the constitution of his new Society. "Give them to me and I'll have them examined,"[9] the Holy Father replied.

Impatient to see France again, and sure of the dispositions of the Holy Father, Fr. Rauzan had the Constitutions sent to the Vatican, and left Fr. Saintyves to take the necessary steps to obtain the Brief of Approval. On February 18, 1834, the Brief was sent out and a few days later the "Society of the Priests of Mercy" were added to the religious institutes of the Sacred Congregation for the Propaganda of the Faith.

It took two months for Fr. Rauzan to reach Paris. He traveled north through Italy, making frequent stops. At the

Holy House of Loreto, he delayed long enough to recommend France and his newly founded Society to the Immaculate Virgin. From Loreto he traveled to Bologna, thence to Milan, where he received with great joy the news that the Society was approved by the Holy See. From Milan, he continued to Savoy, where his significant reputation had inspired several Bishops to request that he establish a foundation in that city for the future Missionaries of the Society. Unfortunately, the Turin government refused to authorize the suggested establishment. Finally, on the eve of the Nativity of the Blessed Mother, he reached his beloved city of Paris. It was a moment of welcome and joy as he left the carriage and was gathered into the arms of his confreres and companions in religion.

The work of the Society was renewed earnestly. For a time, the new home was at Stanislaus College. From there priests were sent on missions from which they returned to rest and share in the religious duties of the house. Later two other foundations were established, one in Bordeaux and the other in Orleans. The house in Bordeaux was at the site of the restoration of St. James's Chapel, where Fr. Rauzan made his first Holy Communion. It was the nucleus of the newly established Order. From here, the Fathers of Mercy left to give missions in parishes throughout the cities.

Orleans was formerly one of the earliest theatres of the apostolate of Rauzan. A church, dedicated to St.

Euverte, Bishop of Orleans and a venerable apostle of the region, stood in the old and noble city. It formerly belonged to the Canons of Sainte Genevieve, who were dispersed in 1792, when the buildings became national property. The Abbey itself belonged to a private party who had transformed the living quarters into a spinning mill. Fr. Rauzan, through negotiations with the Bishop, purchased the Abbey and its dependencies and had them repaired. Toward the latter part of 1836, the Society of the Fathers of Mercy took up residence.

Upon Fr. Rauzan's return to Paris, Bishop Charles de Forbin Janson visited his beloved Superior. Missionary activities were flourishing oversees. Bishop de Forbin Janson revealed his plans to go to America and requested permission to have two of his confreres of the Society of the Fathers of Mercy along. This band of Fathers of Mercy missionaries would tirelessly preach the Gospel to the Catholics of North America.

During this time, Fr. Rauzan followed the groundwork of his beloved missionaries with interest and concern. Ardent and indefatigable, he was firebrand chosen by God, tireless in his efforts to light the torch of Christianity all over the world. He prayed, he blessed, often with a trembling hand; but always with dauntless and abiding faith of paternal love. He would write his children scattered in the mission lands everywhere. The missions were his work, since he had trained the missionaries.

Fr. Rauzan enjoyed a long and full life. From the time he returned from Rome, except for a short trip to

Bordeaux (the city of his birth), he never left Paris again. The words of the Psalmist were reflected in him:

> "Man's days go up to seventy years, and eighty in the more robust; beyond that, there is only trouble and suffering."(Psalm 89:10)

Holiness was a part of him to such an extent that bodily and mental decline could not alter its firmness. He attended community exercises almost to his final hour on earth.

Realizing that his life was quickly ebbing away, Fr. Rauzan called his devoted followers that were in Paris to his side and giving them his last blessing, he encouraged them to be faithful to their priestly virtues and love one another. This blessing he extended to his daughters, the Order of St. Clotilde. The venerable and noble priest offered his beautiful soul to God towards the end of his eighty-ninth year, on Sunday September 5th, 1847. His body was carefully prepared and carried to Bordeaux. He was placed in the church of St. Jacques on September 17, 1847, under the altar of the Blessed Virgin Mary.

The influence of this apostle of mercy cannot be overstated. Fr. Rauzan was so concerned with the spiritual welfare of sinners, and with the necessity of proclaiming the Good News of salvation, that he never spared himself. He faithfully put his talents at the service of the Lord with all simplicity and humility. Perseverance in trials and abandonment to Divine Providence became hallmarks of his life. Within the Catholic Church, the period between 1830 and 1875 shows steady progress in evangelization, both in France and abroad. The missions helped to deepen

Christian life by emphasizing the devotions to the Most Blessed Sacrament, the Sacred Heart of Jesus, and the Immaculate Conception of the Blessed Virgin Mary.

Through the example of Fr. Jean Baptiste Rauzan, many are inspired to preach with courage the Way, the Truth, and the Life. Missionaries follow his example. The members of the Congregation of the Priests of Mercy (Fathers of Mercy), invigorated by the narrative of his life, continue the itinerant preaching apostolate. Through the preaching of parish missions, and the staffing of rural or neglected areas, the Fathers of Mercy call back the prodigal children of the Merciful Father. Their holy founder's life enlightens them as to the true heart of an apostolic missionary, so moved by the mercy of God.

Notes

[1] Pere A. Delaporte, *Vie Du Tres Reverend Pere Jean-Baptiste Rauzan,* (Paris: Maison De La Bonne Presse, 1892), 228.

[2] Jean-Baptiste Lyonnet, *Histoire de Mgr. D'Aviou du Bois-de-Sanzay, successivenent archeveque de Vienne et de Bordeaux,* (Paris: Jacques Lecoffre et Cie, 1847) Vol. 11, 356.

[3] Delaporte, *Vie Du Rauzan,* 6.

[4] Reginald F. Walker, *An Outline History of the Catholic Church,* (Westminster, MD: The Newman Press, 1939), Vol. II, 121.

[5] Delaporte, *Vie Du Rauzan,* 32.

[6] Ibid., 33.

[7] Ibid., 35.

[8] Fanchon Royer, *The Power of Little Children* (Fresno, CA: Academy Library Guild, 1954), 24.

[9] Ibid., 236.

Bibliography

Delaporte, Pere A. *Vie Du Tres Reverend Pere Jean-Baptiste Rauzan.* Paris: Maison De La Bonne Presse, 1892.

Lyonnet, Jean-Baptiste. *Histoire de Mgr. D'Aviou du Bois-de-Sanzay, successivenent archeveque de Vienne et de Bordeaux.* Paris: Jacques Lecoffre et Cie, 1847.

Royer, Fanchon. *The Power of Little Children.* Fresno, CA: Academy Library Guild, 1954.

Walker, Reginald F. *An Outline History of the Catholic Church.* Vol. II. Westminster, MD: The Newman Press, 1939.